This modern art
activity book belongs to

_ _ _ _ _ _ _ _ _ _ _ _ _ _ _

D1579746

Tate kids

MODERN ART

Activity Book

In this book you'll discover ten artworks made by modern and contemporary artists. Each artist's name is **highlighted** so that you know where to start, and the title of their artwork is underlined. The dates (in brackets) are the years when the artworks were made.

Let your imagination expand beyond the pages of this book. For more inspiration visit www.tate.org.uk/kids

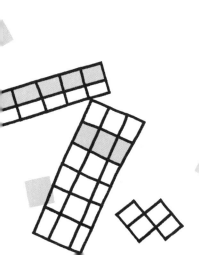

TATE
PUBLISHING

Everyday <u>Extra Ordinary</u>

Choose something from your everyday life and look at it in a different way. Turn it upside down. Flip it up the other way. Look at it in the morning. Look at it at night with a torch. If it lives down low, put it up high. If it usually lives up high, put it under a table. Draw it on the plinth below.

Marcel thought that all chess players were like artists.

Marcel Duchamp

Fountain (1917, replica 1964)

This artwork is an icon of twentieth Century art. It is a urinal from a men's public toilet laid on its back and signed 'R. Mutt.' Marcel elevated objects and made the viewer look at them in a completely different light. He called these artworks 'ready mades.'

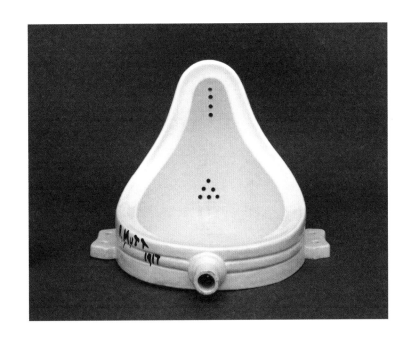

Marcel became a United States citizen in 1955.

Sign Here

Make up a name and make up a signature. It could be an anagram * of your own name.

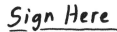

* Anagrams use the same letters but in a different order.

Salvador Dali

Lobster Telephone (1936)

Salvador Dali often put two things (that normally wouldn't be with each other) together with strange results. He made people think differently about each object and how they relate. The images he created often had a dreamlike quality.

Dream Scene

Dreams often don't quite make sense and can contain surprising images. Draw their dreams and then your own in the clouds.

Bad Dream

Good Dream

Mismatch

Find some everyday objects in magazines, cut them out and stack them in to two piles face down. Turn over the pictures to reveal unusual combinations. You could collage them together. Think of interesting ways in which they could be stuck, fused, tied or just balanced.

egg

spanner

Your Dream

Cut it Out

Create a multi-coloured portrait of a tiny animal like a worm, an ant or a spider. Rather than showing what your animal looks like, cut out coloured shapes that match the way it moves, what it sounds like and how it behaves.

Stick or draw it in the space below.

Henri made his cut-outs from bed with the help of an assistant.

Henri Matisse

The Snail (1953)

In the 1940s Henri Matisse became so sick he couldn't paint so he made collages from his bed. His cut-outs were vibrant and expressive. It is said he carved colour. The Snail is an abstract image of a very real thing, the blocks of colour spiral around like a snail's shell.

Henri once designed a huge stained glass window.

The Snail is part of a series of works known as cut-outs.

Colour Combos

Mix the loudest red, the sunniest yellow and an eye-watering purple. Paint whole pieces of paper with a single colour and lay them out to dry. What colour combinations feel fun? Energetic? Sad? Scary?

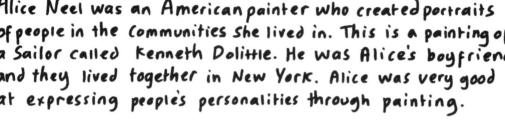

Alice Neel

Kenneth Dolittle (1931)

Alice Neel was an American painter who created portraits of people in the communities she lived in. This is a painting of a sailor called Kenneth Dolittle. He was Alice's boyfriend and they lived together in New York. Alice was very good at expressing people's personalities through painting.

Alice's first solo art exhibition was in Havana, Cuba.

Kenneth cut up and burned 350 of Alice's works.

Strike a Pose

Commission a friend to paint your portrait or take a picture of you and strike a pose. How do you want to look? Strong? Clever? The best? You could use props. Swap roles, swap pictures. Did they capture the inner you?

Inside Out

Take a good look around you. Make a sketch for a painting of somebody in your community. It could be a family member, a friend next door, or even your local shop keeper. Try to express their personality through the marks you make, the colours you use, the clothes they wear, the expression on their face, and their pose.

Alice's nickname was 'Malice'.

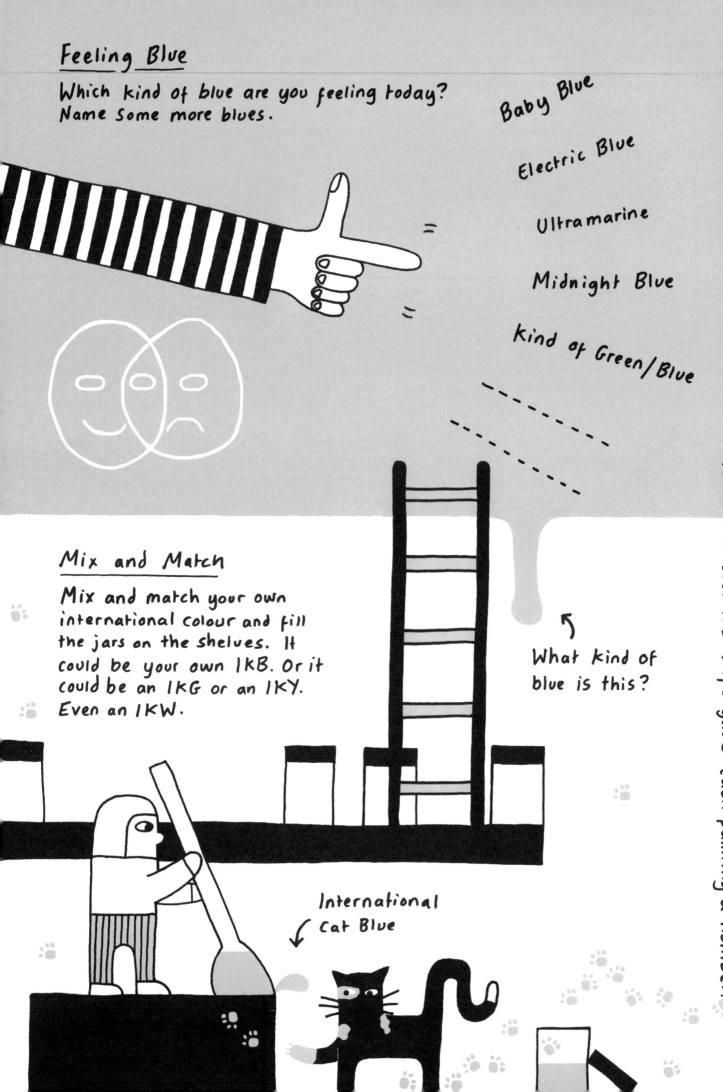

Feeling Blue

Which kind of blue are you feeling today?
Name some more blues.

Baby Blue

Electric Blue

Ultramarine

Midnight Blue

Kind of Green/Blue

Mix and Match

Mix and match your own
international colour and fill
the jars on the shelves. It
could be your own IKB. Or it
could be an IKG or an IKY.
Even an IKW.

What kind of
blue is this?

International
Cat Blue

When he died his wife gave each painting a number.

Yves Klein

IKB 79 (1959)

In the 1940s Yves Klein began to make paintings that were just one colour. He believed that the paintings felt like perfect, pure space because they didn't show recognisable shapes, people or objects. In the 1950s he created 'International Klein Blue (IKB)'- the colour he's now very famous for.

Yves didn't give these paintings titles.

Yves made around 200 paintings in IKB.

You could store your colour in jars and label it.

ICB

Name your colour

_____

OR

_____ for short.

Roy Lichtenstein

Whaam! (1963)

Roy Lichtenstein was a pop artist known for making large versions of panels he found in comic books. For Whaam!, Roy carefully chose an image from a comic book and drew attention to it by blowing it up in scale. This is one of several paintings Roy made about war.

Pop It

Roy's paintings often contain words written in comic book lettering that look the way they sound. Say the word 'pop'. What shape letters would suit this sound? Think about the colours and the marks you make.

You could do the same with

'swoosh'

and 'psssst'

Zoooooooooom

Take a striking image that you would like to highlight from a magazine or newspaper and enlarge it. Draw a grid over your image. Transfer each square to a separate piece of paper.

You could piece it together on your wall ↗

BANG

Draw in any obstacles, characters or object

What's the name of the comic?

Write in any sounds, speech or thoughts.

Blow up a panel from this story.

Eat/Art

Prepare your own paints using food. Check with an adult that your ingredients are safe to use. What do you get when you mix flour with tomato sauce? Or toothpaste with curry powder? Egg with pepper?

Which words will you paint?

Stop?

wiggle? ll

Walk?

MEOW?

Ed Ruscha

Dance ? (1973)

Ed Ruscha often makes graphic paintings that use words to make people laugh. This painting of the phrase 'Dance?' is not made using traditional paint. It is made of a mixture of coffee, egg white, mustard, chilli sauce, ketchup and cheese - Ingredients you'd find in a hot dog or burger joint.

Shuffle?

Two Step?

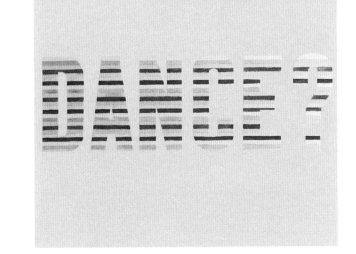

Meal of It

If Ed hadn't made his painting but made dinner instead, what could he have made out of the ingredients?

Ed has also used gunpowder, blood, grass and cherry pie in other works.

Sophie Calle

The Hotel, Room 28, (1981)

In 1981 Sophie Calle took a chambermaid job in a hotel in Venice for three weeks in order to create a series of artworks. As she cleaned the rooms, she looked at the guests' belongings, wrote diary entries and took photographs of what she observed.

Sophie once got a detective to follow her for a day.

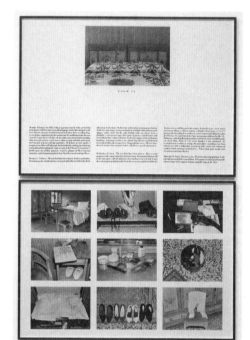

Spy Suit

Imagine that you are a detective. Do you want to blend in or stand out? Formulate a disguise and draw a picture to use as your spy I.D.

Fact / Fiction

Imagine you are a stranger in your own bedroom. Take close-up pictures and write notes about what you see. Take your information and turn it into a fictional spy story.

Detective Notebook

Another artwork in the series is called Room 29.

What would your spy story be called?

Who is Behind Your Door?

Draw the clues in the keyhole that would indicate it's your room.

Wig Out

Design a new hairdo that will change how people view you. Be bold – will you consider curls? Will you add bows or pom-poms? What about a plastic spoon?

Name your hairstyle the _ _ _ _ _ _ _ _

The Giant Quiff →

Wiglette is one of 60 pictures that make up Deluxe.

Ellen Gallagher

Wiglette from DeLuxe (2004-5)

Ellen Gallagher took old advertisements for beauty products aimed at African people and transformed their meaning by adding decorative elements to the surface. In Wiglette, Ellen has used yellow plasticine to enhance the women's hairstyles in her own unique way.

The Vertical Bouffant

← Try out your style!

Ellen lives in both New York and Rotterdam.

Ellen uses unusual materials in her art like velvet, crystals and toy eyeballs.

Outside the Box

Embellish your own series of magazine portraits. Use your imagination - you could use pasta shapes, punch holes or collage fabric. Think about what you are going to exaggerate or reinforce and why.

Meschac Gaba

Museum Shop (1997 - 2002)

Mescha Gaba's artwork, Museum of Contemporary African Art, consists of 12 rooms that you might find in an art gallery or museum. This is his museum shop room. Other artists have provided the stock including bags, postcards and brooches. Meschac's installation shows us that galleries and museums are not only places to look at art. People also come to study, socialise, eat and play.

Meschac has also made a library, music and games room.

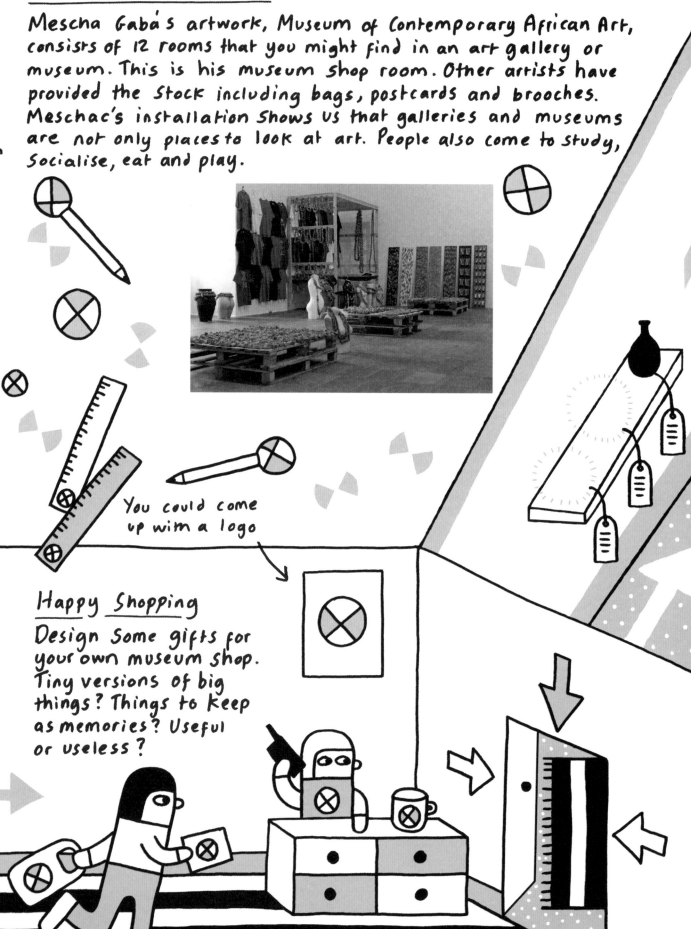

You could come up with a logo

Happy Shopping

Design some gifts for your own museum shop. Tiny versions of big things? Things to keep as memories? Useful or useless?

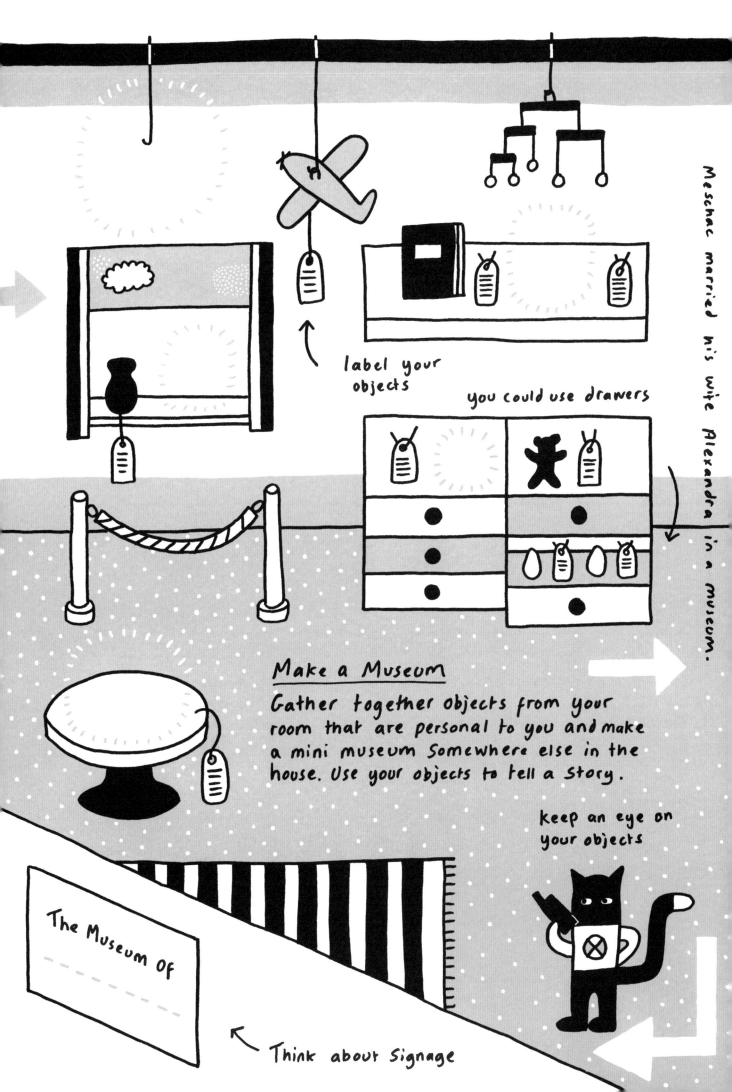

label your objects

you could use drawers

Make a Museum

Gather together objects from your room that are personal to you and make a mini museum somewhere else in the house. Use your objects to tell a story.

keep an eye on your objects

The Museum Of
_ _ _ _ _ _ _ _

← Think about signage

Image captions and copyright credits

First published 2014 by order of the Tate Trustees by
Tate Publishing, a division of Tate Enterprises Ltd,
Millbank, London SW1P 4RG
www.tate.org.uk/publishing

A catalogue record for this book is
available from the British Library
ISBN 978-1-84976-241-0
Distributed in the United States and
Canada by ABRAMS, New York
Library of Congress Control Number applied for

Designed and illustrated by James Lambert
Colour reproduction by DL Imaging
Printed in China by Toppan
Leefung Printing Ltd

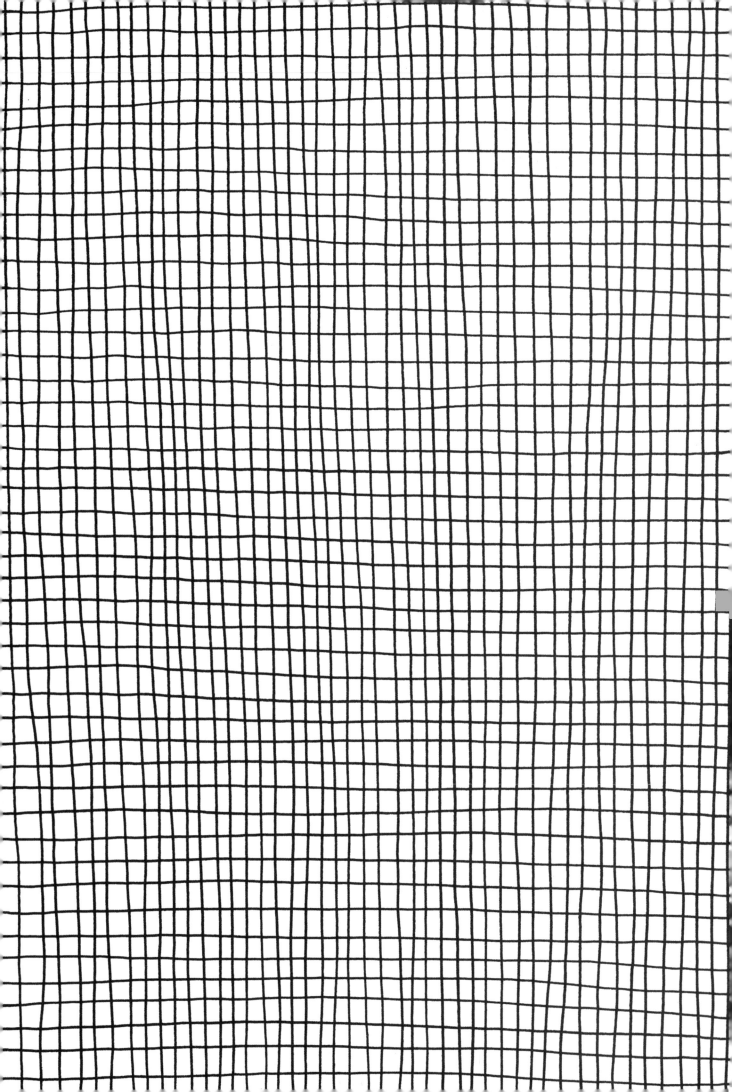